Improve Boys' Reading

Teacher Guidebook

David Grant

www.pearsonschoolsandfecolleges.co.uk

✓ Free online support
✓ Useful weblinks
✓ 24 hour online ordering

0845 630 33 33

Heinemann

Part of Pearson

Heinemann is an imprint of Pearson Education Limited, Edinburgh Gate, Harlow, Essex, CM20 2JE.

www.pearsonschoolsandfecolleges.co.uk

Heinemann is a registered trademark of Pearson Education Limited

Text © David Grant 2011
Typeset by Emily Hunter-Higgins
Original illustrations © Emily Hunter-Higgins
Cover design by Tony Richardson at Wooden Ark Ltd

The right of David Grant to be identified as authors of this work has been asserted by him in accordance with the Copyright, Designs and Patents Act 1988.

First published 2011

15 14 13 12 11
10 9 8 7 6 5 4 3 2 1

British Library Cataloguing in Publication Data
A catalogue record for this book is available from the British Library

ISBN 9780435049645

Printed by Ashford Digital

Acknowledgements
We are grateful to the following for permission to reproduce copyright material:

Data on page 1, 11, 13, 14, 26: Raising Boys' Achievement (Research Report RR636) Department for Education and Skills, 2005; Data on page 4: Clark C., Osborne, S. and Akerman, R. (2008). Young People's Self-Perceptions as Readers: An investigation including family, peer and school influences. London: National Literacy Trust; Data on page 5: Young Australians Reading: from keen to reluctant readers (2001) Prepared for the Australian Centre for Youth Literature and the Audience and Market Development Division of the Australia Council by Woolcott Research Pty Ltd. By kind permission of the Australia Council. All rights reserved; Data on page 6: Clark, C and Foster, A. (2005). Children's and Young People's Reading Habits and Preferences: The who, what, why, where and when. London: National Literacy Trust; Data in section 'The importance of choice', page 9: Clark, C and Pythian-Sence, C. (2008). Interesting choice: The (relative) importance of choice and interest in reader engagement. London: National Literacy Trust; Data on page 15: Using the National Healthy School Standard to Raise Boys' Achievement Department of Health, 2003; Data on page 46: Teaching Effective Vocabulary Department for Children, Schools and Families, 2008; Data on page 50: Effective Teaching of Inference Skills for Reading Department for Children, Schools and Families, 2008.

Every effort has been made to contact copyright holders of material reproduced in this book. Any omissions will be rectified in subsequent printings if notice is given to the publishers.

Pearson Education Limited is not responsible for the content of any external internet sites. It is essential for tutors to preview each website before using it in class so as to ensure that the URL is still accurate, relevant and appropriate. We suggest that tutors bookmark useful websites and consider enabling students to access them through the school/college intranet.

Contents

Introduction

The purpose of this guide is, as the title suggests, to improve boys' reading – and specifically to engage boys (and, indeed, any reluctant readers) in reading fiction.

Why do we teach fiction to students? Why do we care if students are reading fiction or not? Because it broadens students' experience of the power of words to explore and change our lives, our thoughts and feelings, our humanity?

Well, yes, that's important. But actually I think there's a far more powerful reason to get youngsters reading fiction: it's fun. And those students who stand firm against fiction are missing out on the fun.

This guide is not going to turn the steadfast book-refuser into the Booker Prize winner of tomorrow. Hopefully, however, it will give you some ideas that can help your most bibliophobic students turn the task of decoding into the pleasure of reading, rebuild their confidence and faith in fiction and set them on the path to becoming a reader.

I hope it helps.

David Grant

Reading for boys: the story so far

The trouble with boys

The gender gap has been an educational cliché for some years. In national tests, boys' level of achievement is consistently below that of girls. Results in national tests have improved over time – and yet the gap between boys and girls remains static. There has been a significant improvement in girls' performance in the traditionally boy-friendly GCSEs of Science and Mathematics, yet boys have not made a similar improvement in the traditionally female bastions of English, Modern Languages and Humanities.

The Raising Boys' Achievement project (RBA), conducted by the University of Cambridge Faculty of Education, noted one significant element that holds boys back: 'Boys' lack of engagement with literacy has been identified as

'Boys' lack of engagement with literacy has been identified as one of the most significant factors in accounting for their lower attainment in relation to girls.'

one of the most significant factors in accounting for their lower attainment in relation to girls.' (*Raising Boys' Achievement*, DfES).

The National Literacy Trust's research paper, *Literacy: State of the Nation*, notes the long-term impact of low literacy levels beyond the classroom: one in six people in the United Kingdom – five million adults – struggle with literacy. The NLT's measure of struggling is having a literacy level below that expected of an 11-year-old. Clearly, poor literacy is not a recent phenomenon.

The Department for Education's Every Child a Reader (ECaR)[1] programme identifies significant social consequences arising from poor literacy skills:

- 70% of pupils permanently excluded from school have difficulties in basic literacy skills.

- 25% of young offenders are said to have reading skills below those of the average seven-year-old.

- 60% of the prison population is said to have difficulties in basic literacy skills.

It is perhaps worth adding to this picture that approximately 80% of students excluded from primary and secondary schools are boys – and that 95% of the prison population is male.[2,3]

[1] see http://www.everychildachancetrust.org/ecar/background/why.cfm

[2] see http://www.justice.gov.uk/publications/docs/pop-in-custody-aug2010.pdf

[3] see http://www.education.gov.uk/rsgateway/DB/SFR/s000733/sfr21-2007.pdf

Clearly, social deprivation is a factor in exclusion and crime, but it is hard to deny that boys' literacy levels – and, at its root, their engagement with literacy skills – is an issue that must be addressed.

The importance of literacy – and in particular boys' literacy – is not simply a question of educational achievement, of 'results'. It is a key factor in the health, wealth and happiness of individuals and the society in which they – and we – live.

What *is* a reluctant reader?

The National Literacy Trust (NLT) report *Young People's Self-Perception as Readers* (2008) presents a perhaps surprising picture of young people's reading habits – but a familiar picture of boys' attitudes to reading.

The majority of students associated reading with positive feelings, such as feeling calm and happy. A third of pupils said that reading makes them feel bored. More girls than boys said that reading makes them feel calm and happy.

When the survey asked students to imagine someone who enjoys reading, most pupils viewed readers positively and as achievers. A third of pupils believed that readers are geeks/nerds, while a quarter perceived readers to be boring. Girls tended to see readers as 'clever/intelligent' and 'someone who will do well in life'. Boys tended to regard readers as 'geeky/nerds'.

The survey asked 1,614 students from 29 primary and secondary schools to define themselves as 'readers' or 'non-readers'. Over 70% of students defined themselves as readers. Those who defined themselves as readers read a wide range of texts and were far more likely to read fiction. And yet 11% of the non-readers still read fiction, 66% read magazines, 52% read websites, 49% read blogs/networking websites and 43% read emails.

This seems to suggest that when a student says they 'do not like reading' and therefore do not read, what they mean is that they do not like reading fiction – and don't read it.

A similar study in Australia also questioned students on whether they felt reading for pleasure was 'easy': 68% of girls and 57% of boys felt reading was easy. The report concluded: 'The fact that 43% of boys do not associate reading for pleasure with being easy confirms the need for focus on improvement of reading skills amongst boys in particular.'[4]

There is no one definition of the term 'reluctant reader'. It can refer to those who are below the level of functional literacy, defined by the OECD as those who cannot 'engage in all those activities in which literacy is required for effective functioning of his group and community and also for...his own and the community's development'.

The term 'reluctant reader' can equally refer to those who have achieved functional literacy but shy away from reading – those who can but won't read.

The *Young Australians Reading* survey suggests that as such a high percentage of boys (43%) do not describe reading for pleasure as 'easy', this is not simply a problem of functional illiteracy. The majority of these students can read and can decode text and extract meaning – but not easily, perhaps not fluently. So even for those children who have achieved

[4] Young Australians Reading: From Keen to Reluctant Readers, 2001; see http://www.australiacouncil.gov.au/research/literature/reports_and_publications/ young_australians_reading

functional literacy, the inherent relationship between the practice of reading and reading improvement becomes a vicious circle: those who find reading difficult will not read and will therefore continue to find reading difficult – and boring.

The NLT survey, *Children's and Young People's Reading Habits and Preferences* (2005), asked over 8,000 young people about their favourite genre of fiction. The top five for boys were:

- adventure (64.7%)
- comedy (58.1%)
- horror/ghost (54%)
- war/spy related (47.5%)
- crime/detective (43.7%).

Significantly, the results for girls reported the same top three genres.

The survey also reported its findings according to reading enjoyment. Those who reported enjoying reading 'very much' or 'quite a lot' were designated enthusiastic readers. Those who reported enjoying reading 'a bit' or 'not at all' were designated reluctant readers.

Reluctant readers' favourite genres of fiction were reported as:

- horror/ghost (60.9%)
- adventure (60.2%)
- comedy (54.4%)

- crime/detective (37.8%)

- real teenage fiction (32.1%).

It seems that genre is not a significant point of division between the enthusiastic and the reluctant reader.

All the children surveyed were asked to rate their own proficiency in reading on a scale of 1 (poor) to 10 (very proficient). While the vast majority of enthusiastic readers rated themselves between 7 and 10, the vast majority of reluctant readers rated themselves between 5 and 8. While this is a self-diagnosis, it does strongly suggest that the majority of reluctant readers are aliterate, not illiterate: they choose not to read rather than being unable to read.

Why do reluctant readers make this choice? The NLT survey reports that while 74% of enthusiastic readers cited the main reason for reading as 'because it's fun', the same response was returned by just 19% of reluctant readers.

Reluctant readers were also significantly more likely than enthusiastic readers to agree with the following statements:

- Reading is for girls.

- Reading is boring.

- Reading is hard.

- I cannot find books that interest me.

- I do not read as well as other pupils in my class.

A picture emerges of the typical, or perhaps stereotypical, reluctant reader: he is male, finds reading challenging, has little confidence in his reading and does not value reading.

Reluctant readers were also asked what would make them read more. The top five responses given were that they would read more if:

- I enjoyed it more (61%)
- it was about interesting subjects (36%)
- I had more time (35%)
- books had more pictures (32%)
- stories were shorter (29%).

This could suggest that if reluctant readers could discover shorter, illustrated fiction that centred on their interests, then they might find more time for reading – and enjoy it more.

The importance of choice

How do you choose a book for the classroom – and how do young people choose a book to read for pleasure?

The NLT paper, *Interesting Choice*, explores 'the (relative) importance of choice and interest in reader engagement'. It emphasises the role that a student's interest in a text has in their willingness and ability to decode and comprehend it:

> *Generally, interest has been shown to affect emotional engagement (e.g. Schiefele, 1999), persistence with a task (Vollmeyer and Rheinberg, 2000), and to influence learning, attention, and comprehension (Schiefele, 1999). With regards to reading, children who are interested in the texts comprehend them better than children with similar reading skills but lower interest. Interest is also related to persistence to read challenging text passages (e.g. Naceur and Schiefele, 2005).*
>
> **(*Interesting Choice*, NLT, 2008)**

While it is unsurprising that interest is closely linked to a reader's motivation, this study goes on to explore topics that research suggests will create interest and engagement. It cites Schank (with some caution), who asserts in 'Interestingness: Controlling Inferences' (1979) that concepts such as death, violence and sex can be considered 'absolute interests', which are almost guaranteed to capture

9

interest. It goes on to cite Zahoric's 'Elementary and secondary teachers' reports of how they make learning interesting' (1996), who adds the rather nebulous 'life issues' to this list of topics. Zahoric asserts that 'young adults, who can be particularly difficult to engage in reading, may be surprised to find texts that explore these themes, and may be motivated to read by these topics.'

The study then suggests that **interest** is a key factor in encouraging young people to read. In fact, interest may be a stronger factor than whether the text is at an appropriate reading level:

> *A highly motivated pupil may persevere through a challenging text, just as an unmotivated pupil may disengage from a readable, but personally uninteresting text.*

> (*Interesting Choice,* NLT, 2008)

Clearly choosing a book that is appropriate to the reader's ability is not the only significant factor in engaging readers.

The value of talk

Engaging young people's interest in reading is, then, not simply a question of placing a readable text in front of them. It is a part of the English teacher's role to select texts that are not only appropriate but also engaging. Furthermore, it is not the English teacher's role simply to teach reading, but it is their role to teach the **enjoyment** of reading.

In the University of Cambridge Faculty of Education paper, *Raising Boys' Achievement* (RBA), the writers outline one group of schools in which the aim became concentrated not so much on 'a concern about *teaching reading,* but a need to focus on encouraging boys to become *successful and satisfied readers'.*

The report notes that this was achieved in a number of ways, including 'having a wide range of texts available to stimulate and sustain pupils' interest and to build confidence through paired reading schemes'.

However, it notes the absolute importance of discussion: the need for teachers to 'give pupils space to talk and reflect about their reading, to share ideas about the text and what was enjoyable in it. When this happened and teachers had the confidence to develop an integrated approach to literacy, the standards of reading of many boys improved markedly, sometimes by twice that expected within national test parameters.'

This suggests that the discussion of text – purposeful interaction between students and teacher and focused discussion among students – can engage and encourage students to value not only their reading but also their response to it. Reading, therefore, becomes not a task or challenge in itself but a stimulus to individual expression.

Learning styles

The RBA report explores the role of different learning styles in some detail. It considers the role of multiple intelligences (Gardner, 1983, 1999) and the more specific focus on Visual, Auditory and Kinaesthetic learning (Smith, 2001).

That boys favour kinaesthetic learning has long been accepted. The report, however, does not entirely support this:

> *We have found little evidence, for example, to support the notion that the dominant learning style of boys differs from those of girls, and that more boys (than girls) favour kinaesthetic learning.... students [need to] understand that, as individuals, they have different learning styles, some of which (e.g. visual, auditory or kinaesthetic) may be more prominent than others, but that to be effective learners, they must be able to access different learning styles at different times.*
>
> **(*Raising Boys' Achievement*, DfES)**

However, the report notes that, in one school taking part in the study, there was one group of students for whom kinaesthetic learning was particularly appropriate. This group, comprised mainly of boys, were those students whom their teachers characterised 'as falling into one of a number of "bad behaviour" categories and in danger of "under-achieving" (for example, those said by teachers to be "disillusioned and negative about teachers and school" or those who were "disorganised")'. (*Raising Boys' Achievement*, DfES)

It could perhaps be argued that this characterisation is similar in many ways to that of the reluctant reader. The report also notes that '"[m]odel" students, in contrast, and both male and female teachers, displayed a marked tendency to visual learning.' It is, perhaps, that kinaesthetic activities are far less prevalent in most classrooms – and not least in the English classroom – than those visual activities that the teacher is likely to find so effective as a learner.

The RBA report does not, though, advocate an over-emphasis on any one learning style or on shaping the curriculum and its delivery for boys:

> *Our research does not support the notion that there is a case for boy-friendly pedagogies. Pedagogies that appeal to and engage boys are equally girl-friendly. They characterise quality teaching, and as such are just as suitable and desirable for girls as for boys.*

> **(*Raising Boys' Achievement,* DfES)**

A vast range of literature notes teaching strategies that are likely to engage boys. An effective summary is given in *Using the National Healthy School Standard to Raise Boys' Achievement* (Wilson, Gary, 2003, DfES).

From *Using the National Healthy School Standard to Raise Boys'
Achievement,* Department for Education and Skills, 2003:
'...boys are...given the opportunity to be more responsive and
achieve more because:

- Work is delivered in bite-sized chunks and is time-limited
- Lessons are broken down into a number of different
  activities, including more active learning opportunities,
  eg drama, investigation, research or the use of information
  communication technology (ICT)
- The work feels relevant to them, with a real purpose and a
  real audience
- Work is delivered with pace and there is a real sense of
  direction and progression
- There is an element of challenge or competition, with
  short-term goals
- Social learning is allowed – from simply sitting with
  someone who can help them discuss and reflect on ideas, to
  well organised and structured group work
- A period of reflection/review is allowed at the end of lessons
- Positive feedback is given regularly.'

A list of effective teaching strategies for all students,
regardless of gender, might look very similar to those listed
to raise boys' achievement. Good teaching takes account of
the learners' needs, but the strategies and approaches that
characterise successful teaching and achieve successful
learning are universal.

A summary

- Literacy is a key factor in boys' under-achievement with significant consequences for individual academic achievement and for society as a whole.

- The reluctant reader may be functionally literate but does not necessarily find reading easy. The reluctant reader is unlikely to be a fluent reader, which may significantly reduce their engagement with text.

- The reader's interest in a text can be a more significant factor in their engagement than it matching their reading ability precisely. Interest can create motivation and perseverance.

- Once functional literacy is achieved, the teaching of reading should focus not on improving reading per se but on the creation of enjoyment in reading. Discussion can be a key factor in this.

- Effective teachers and learners recognise the value of a balanced variety of learning styles in the classroom, including kinaesthetic learning. Teaching strategies that appeal to boys are just as likely to appeal to girls and, as such, are characteristic of good teaching.

Why *HEROES*?

HEROES is a series of novels and plays commissioned to respond to the needs of all reluctant readers – but particularly boys.

Each title in the series aims to engage students in the reading of a play or novel; to build their interest, confidence, enjoyment and sense

> *Engagement* to *build confidence* to bring *improvement.*

of success in reading; and ultimately to make them better readers. In short, *engagement* to *build confidence* to *bring improvement*.

The titles

As discussed previously, the National Literacy Trust's survey *Children's and Young People's Reading Habits and Preferences* (2005) suggested that reluctant readers would read more if novels were shorter, more interesting and had more pictures.

The titles in the *HEROES* series are, on average, around 25,000 words – perhaps half the length of a typical children's or young adult novel.[5] Pace and tension are kept high with cliffhangers aplenty to keep the pages turning.

The range of genres in the series has been selected for its appeal to reluctant readers – and, in particular, reluctant male readers: adventure, horror, ghost stories and crime, centring on young male protagonists and told with humour.

Each title includes a short non-fiction article that is thematically linked to the story, placing the narrative in a 'real world' context, and adding interest and relevance for the reluctant reader.

Each title has been tested by real readers to ensure accessibility for students who are functionally literate but not necessarily fluent readers.

[5] assuming a typical children's or young adult novel is usually 40,000–60,000 words

The resources

To support delivery in the classroom, an ActiveTeach resource is available for each title in the *HEROES* series. Again, these have been specifically written and designed in response to research on the needs of, and strategies appropriate to, reluctant readers.

The ActiveTeach consists of 18 – 20 lesson plans, each structured with a starter activity, reading selection, main activity, quiz and bonus question. A homework task is suggested in every third lesson. Seventeen lessons are allocated for the reading of the novel or play. Two lessons focus on a reading and writing assessment.

Tasks are presented in a series of clearly written, on-screen instructions. Detailed teacher's notes accompany each activity. A vast range of features ensures each activity is directed firmly at the needs of the reluctant reader:

- Throughout your teaching of the text, multimedia resources support and direct students' learning. These resources include video footage of the author, specially commissioned illustrations, relevant images and animation.

- Two on-screen versions of the novel are provided. In one, the text is plain. In the other, the dialogue of each character is colour coded to support a teacher reading the bulk of the narrative aloud and students reading the dialogue of a particular character.

- Many of the activities are set within an imaginative scenario to create a sense of purpose. For example, drama activities are preceded by video footage of the author inviting students to audition for a film version of the novel or play.

- Kinaesthetic learning is strongly represented in a range of drama and discussion tasks and in the supporting materials for reading and writing activities.

- Discussion and collaboration play a central role. Students are given frequent opportunities to respond to the novel in teacher-led interactions and in closely focused group discussion tasks, each with a specific outcome.

- Written tasks are highly structured, thoroughly supported, and designed to immerse students in the world of the novel or play. Empathetic responses ask students to place themselves in characters' shoes; script writing tasks place students in the author's shoes; review writing gives students the opportunity to express a full and honest response to their reading.

- Competition is a key element in the resources. In recognising that competition can impede collaboration, each activity is presented within the context of a team competition. Students are therefore rewarded for collaboration. Teachers are asked to divide their class into two teams that will compete throughout the study of the text. Points are awarded for participation and effective, engaged responses.

- Time limits are a key competitive and motivational feature. The majority of activities feature an on-screen timer to encourage students to participate, to remain on-task and to complete the task. The timer can also be used to limit feedback time, encouraging swift, relevant and uninterrupted responses.

- A comprehension quiz is included in each lesson. The teams are presented with a set of on-screen questions in turn. Each question has three multiple choice answers. Progress is monitored by an on-screen animation. The first team to answer all six questions correctly wins points. The quiz, then, monitors and assesses understanding – and promotes students' careful attention during the reading of the text.

- The team with the most points at the end of the lesson has the opportunity to double their lesson's points by answering a bonus question. This question is posed by the author of the play or novel. This bonus point opportunity promotes excitement and encourages participation throughout the lesson.

Suggestions for management and extension of all of the above features are discussed in the next section.

Approaches

Talking about reading

Reluctant readers are often all too conscious of their lack of
confidence and lack of enjoyment in reading.

Time spent discussing and surveying your group's reading
habits can help you identify – and perhaps improve – students'
attitudes and assumptions.

Many students who consider themselves non-readers will
frequently read newspapers, magazines, websites and so on
(see NLT survey, page 6). A small number may even read fiction,
albeit infrequently.

Ask your students whether they consider themselves to
be 'readers'. Ask them what they read and how frequently.
A survey on a single sheet of A4 (see suggested template
following) will achieve a faster, simpler and more honest
response. A quick flick through the completed surveys should
immediately reveal dominant attitudes to reading and, in
particular, to fiction.

Reading survey template

Your name _____

Are you a reader or a non-reader? _____

How often do you read the following?
Often? Occasionally? Or never?

- Fiction books _____
- Non-fiction books _____
- Magazines _____
- Comics/graphic novels _____
- Newspapers _____
- Catalogues _____
- Websites _____
- Social networking sites _____
- Emails _____
- Text messages _____

Which of the following kinds of fiction would you prefer to read?
Tick up to three boxes:

- ☐ Adventure
- ☐ Animal stories
- ☐ Comedy
- ☐ Crime/detective
- ☐ Ghost/horror
- ☐ Realistic teenage stories
- ☐ Romance
- ☐ Sci fi/fantasy
- ☐ Sports
- ☐ War/spy stories
- ☐ Other

Figure 1: Reading survey template

Ask the class to expand on their preferences and habits – but make it clear that use of the phrase 'because it's boring' will result in an unthinkable penalty. Students should be encouraged to articulate *why* they find fiction (or other forms or specific genres) difficult or unappealing.

Ask your students to share positive experiences of fiction – or more specifically 'stories'. Who was read to as a young child – either by their parents or their teacher? The likelihood is that all students have experienced – and enjoyed – the pleasure of listening to a story, whether at bedtime or sitting in a circle on the carpet of their primary school classroom. Which stories have they enjoyed?

Why do these students who once enjoyed listening to stories find that they do not enjoy reading stories for themselves? Is it the mechanics, the *process* of reading, that impedes their enjoyment? Or perhaps they no longer find relevance in the stories that are available to them?

Ask students to compile a list of 'ingredients' that might tempt them into reading a fiction book.

- What kind of protagonist or hero would they like to read about?

- What kinds of situation would they like to see that protagonist in?

- In what kinds of setting – when and where – would they like to see that protagonist?

- How would they like the story to make them *feel?*

Aim to achieve the following from your discussion:

- Your students become aware that they *are* readers, even if they do not initially consider themselves to be.

- Your students become more aware of their reading preferences – and the obstacles they encounter in their reading.

- Your students acknowledge that at some point in their lives they have enjoyed reading or listening to fiction – and you insist that they can do again!

Finally, introduce the novel or play that you and your group are going to read together. Emphasise *any* elements in the story that your students identified as ingredients that might tempt them to read fiction. Hopefully there will be more than one.

Be clear on *your* intentions in choosing this book. You hope to engage them in a narrative. You hope to build their confidence in reading. And ultimately you hope to develop their reading skills, to make them 'successful and satisfied readers' (*Raising Boys' Achievement,* DfES).

Choosing the novel

Offering your students a choice of novels or plays for whole class study is a luxury open to few English teachers. The stock cupboard is rarely that full.

The important decision is taken at the buying stage. The book you buy will be the title that your budget dictates you will use with that year and ability group for some time to come.

As noted earlier, readability is perhaps not the primary concern when looking to engage reluctant readers. Indeed, if you are hoping to improve your students' reading, there does need to be an element of challenge. However, it's some comfort to know that your students have some hope of accessing the text you are considering. Your students' reading ages should be available from your SENCo.

To assess your chosen novel or play, there are a number of readability tests that you can apply to an extract. Searching for 'online readability tool' in your preferred search engine should produce a number of automated reading age calculators. Type or paste in your extract and the calculator will probably return a bewildering array of vastly disparate results using different methods: reading ages spanning up to four or even five years, in my experience. Taking an average may give you some idea as to whether your chosen text is appropriate. Alternatively, your SENCo may have time on their hands and be more than happy to reliably calculate the text's reading age. Or you may want to rely purely on your common sense, experience and expertise.

Readability aside, what other considerations should influence your choice of text? If your ultimate concern is engaging reluctant readers, then those factors that you might take into account for more enthusiastic readers can be discounted: the beauty of the prose, the range of issues explored, the depth of characterisation, the opportunities for Ofsted-inspector-dazzling activities[6]...

For the reluctant reader, your ultimate guide is whether the story will have the class pounding the desks, demanding you read the next chapter. This can be the response to a story with incredible narrative pace, intense relevance to your students' lives or dreams, irresistible escapism, hugely appealing characters and settings – and ideally all of the above. Remember, it may not be the novel that would have you pounding on a desk (not for the right reasons at least) but you are not a reluctant reader who urgently needs to be engaged in the essential skill of reading.

[6] Estyn-inspector-dazzling if teaching in Wales, HMIE-inspector-dazzling in Scotland, ETI-inspector-dazzling in Northern Ireland

Reading the novel

Reading around the class can be a dispiriting activity for all concerned. Listening to a class of reluctant readers slogging their way through a paragraph or a page each, it becomes very apparent where these students' reluctance comes from.

The reluctant (but functional) reader is able to decode the words and say them aloud. But expression, pace and engagement and meaning are frequently absent. The story stops being a story; it becomes one word after another, one painful step after another up a very steep hill. I defy even the most avid reader to enjoy their favourite novel when read in a mono-paced monotone.

More importantly, is the student reader understanding what they are reading? Are those students who are about to read actually listening to the story? Or are they too busy worrying that it must be nearly their turn for the ritual humiliation of reading aloud? If this is so, then as you embark on reading around the class, all but one of your students are panicking, one is reading aloud, and none of them is listening. Engagement in the fast paced, gripping narrative that you have so carefully chosen is lost.

'Popcorn reading' has been considered an effective method of reading around the class while maintaining students' attention. The teacher starts the reading, then passes the reading on to a randomly selected student who then has the privilege of nominating the next reader, and so on. Each student reads a self-selected or teacher-set amount of text aloud. Alternatively, the teacher can select the student by randomly picking an ice lolly stick or wooden spatula on each of which is written a student's name.

The problem with popcorn reading is it accentuates the element of combat and the risk of humiliation: students are encouraged to 'follow' the story so that they are not caught out when it's their turn. Keeping up – rather than comprehension or enjoyment – becomes the chief objective.

In short, reading around the classroom can kill any story stone dead. And yet what are the alternatives? If you read the story to them (with all the enthusiasm and pace you can muster), then they are not reading – and that's what they're supposed to be getting better at, isn't it?

Yes and no.

No, they're not reading but they may, hopefully, be 'following'. Even if they're not 'following', they are almost certainly listening – and listening to an expert reader modelling the art of reading.

Indeed, there is a lot to be said for the pure experience of shared reading: ten minutes at the start of each lesson in which the teacher reads a novel to the class over a number of weeks. No activities, no direct teaching or learning, just the pure enjoyment of reading for pleasure and discussion of the issues it raises.

Whatever and however you're reading, does it matter that some of your students are not 'following'? Or that one or two may be reading ahead? No. If your students are engaged – and there is nothing that engages students like a well-chosen, well-read story – then that is all that matters. Your first challenge with these students is to give them a story that they will enjoy. And anything that can prevent them enjoying that story – including reading it for themselves – is a negative.

Removing the process of reading the novel entirely from students does, however, seem counter-productive. There is a range of methods to get students reading in class that can be used periodically – perhaps two or three times each during the course of reading a novel – without pain.

One method is for the teacher to read the narrative while the dialogue for each character is allocated to a student. If the students are relatively confident readers, then this can work well. However, in longer passages of dialogue it can be easier to lose track of who is saying what. *Note: An on-screen version of the HEROES novels is available on the ActiveTeach with each character's dialogue highlighted and colour-coded to support this method.*

Reducing the audience in front of which you ask students to 'sight-read' text can help. Ask students to read a chapter or a specific number of pages with a partner or in a small group. Encourage them to pause during reading for discussion, whether to support each other in decoding unfamiliar language, to discuss their comprehension or to respond to the narrative.

It can also be effective to ask students to read short passages independently and then ask for their general or specific response – preferably verbally, and preferably to the whole class to assure you of their understanding and engagement.

It is, however, possible to achieve whole class reading with minimised panic and pain. Divide the chapter(s) you want students to read into chunks of two or three pages. Divide your class into groups of three or four. Give each chunk of reading and each group a letter – A, B, C, etc. Give groups 10 or 15 minutes to practise reading their particular chunk – either by dividing their pages between them or allocating dialogue and narrative to different group members. Emphasise the qualities you are looking for in their reading: clarity, fluency and expression to engage their listeners in the story they are telling. Ask Group A to begin reading and Group B to follow seamlessly on, and so on to the end of the chapter(s). When all the groups have read, praise those students who were particularly clear, or fluent, or expressive. Above all, praise the whole class for reading aloud.

Competition

Boys love competition. And, no matter what anyone might say, so do girls. Competition can motivate learning. But the value of competition is not purely in its motivational powers but in the explicitness of its rewards. Praise is good. Students like it. But make it more explicit and tangible with the awarding of points, and students like it even more. Students feel not only that they have achieved something but also that they have earned, and deserved to earn, something. The hope is that students will come to recognise what success feels like and may even turn from reading for explicit reward to reading for implicit reward – readers who enjoy reading and achieving success in the classroom.

However, making learning competitive can introduce as many problems as it solves.

In any competition there will be winners and there will be those who fail to win: the losers. Those students whose reading confidence is already fragile do not need to have it crushed further by failing again. And yet the motivational power of competition is difficult to deny. The answer lies, I think, in the careful management of the competition.

Creating a team competition that runs during the course of your work on a text can minimise individual responsibility. Emphasise the team's responsibility in supporting each other – even those students who do not directly achieve success should be considered to have contributed to it. Be clear that points will be awarded to each team for individual achievements *and* for the quality of their teamwork; bickering over who let the team down will result in you deducting points.

How do you divide your class into two teams? It depends on the class. Student-selected friendship groups can help team spirit. Dividing them randomly by, say, date of birth can add an exciting frisson of danger to the whole process – but do bear in mind that these teams will have to work together for the next few weeks and you may tire of the frisson.

Dividing them by overall ability can help to keep the competition even – or, if you know the group well, by their specific strengths and weaknesses: divide the stronger readers, the more confident speakers, the harder workers (and so on) evenly between the teams.

For ease of management, the best thing is physically to divide the class down the middle: everyone to the left is on one team, everyone to the right is on the other. Introducing a new seating plan just before starting the text – a seating plan in which you have carefully placed a balance of students who you feel will work and succeed together – will help.

Decide which activities in your reading of the novel will be rewarded with points. Perhaps the best approach is to award points for everything: activities, reading aloud, behaviour, in fact anything that happens between the start and end of each lesson. Scatter points like confetti wherever possible – making it clear that you value each and every achievement for which students are being rewarded. Differentiate your rewards: one student may achieve a point for reading a page beautifully, another for reading a sentence haltingly. There is no need to broadcast how many points are being awarded for what: your picking up your pen and making a note on that piece of paper will soon come to be seen and recognised as a reward.

At the end of each lesson, declare one team that day's winner. Use the number of lessons each team has 'won' as the overall, running score. This makes it much easier to ensure that the battle is fairly even to the end – especially if you bear in mind the need to keep things even when you're handing out the points. Once one team feels that, no matter how many battles they might win, they have lost the war, then motivation is lost with it. If you're lucky, you might even be able to engineer a draw.

Starters

An engaging start to the lesson can be essential in immersing readers in a story. Here are just a few ideas to recap the story so far, to consolidate, develop and explore understanding or to think about the story to come. All involve minimal preparation for you – and minimal writing and maximum thinking and discussion for students.

1. Cover story

Before starting the reading, ask students to look at the book cover, the book title and the blurb on the back. What kind of story is this? What kinds of characters and setting will it have? What do they think will happen? How will it end?

Give students five minutes to note their thoughts independently or in pairs.

Take feedback, praising any comments that show some engagement with the task and with the story they are about to begin.

2. Images

Images can be particularly engaging and motivating in supporting prediction. If illustrations are available (the ActiveTeach for each *HEROES* title features illustrations of key moments in the novel), present these to students at appropriate points, inviting their predictions for the section they are about to read. Otherwise, with a little imagination and planning, you can find relevant images on the internet.

For example, prior to the Children's March chapters in *i-SSASSINS*, present students with an image of a major demonstration in London, preferably one showing signs of disorder. Ask students to predict how this could be connected to the story and how the story will develop.

3. Brief the illustrator

This can be used for recap. Ask students to 'play publisher' and suggest key scenes which they would ask an illustrator to draw to accompany the last lesson's reading.

For example, having read about the spooky house that Danny and his dad move into at the start of *Ghost Game*, how would students want and expect the house to look? Compile a list of ideas on the board.

4. Odd one out

This is an excellent way of prompting thought and discussion. On the whiteboard, present three ideas, events or characters to students. Ask them to note down which one they consider the odd one out and, most importantly, *why*.

For example, in *Chamber of Nothing*, present students with three characters, each of whom can be considered the odd one out: Mrs Presley (she is a non-believer), Mr Young (a man, younger and kinder), The Guide (scary, supernatural).

Hopefully your students will come up with a range of answers and reasons that effectively and immediately recap and summarise the narrative, characters, and so on. However, they may take some persuading that there is not – and never was – any one correct answer.

5. Snap

This is a variation of Odd one out. Present students with a series of pairs of characters from the novel. Is there any connection between them? Or a contrast/conflict? If so, and your ears and your classroom management can stand it, ask students to shout 'Snap' (or just put up their hands) and name that connection or contrast. There may well be several possible answers, i.e. a connection (they're married) and a conflict (but they hate each other).

Sum up by highlighting the pushes and pulls, the relationships and conflicts, without which the story would halt.

6. The headline game

This is a great way to summarise previous reading. Give students, working in pairs or groups of three, five minutes to think of a television news headline to sum up the events either of the novel so far or of the previous chapter. Explain to each group that when you point at them they should read their headline aloud. Begin feedback with (in your most gravitas-laden voice) 'Good evening, this is the six o'clock news', then point your way around the classroom until each headline has been heard.

7. The handbag game

This can help students explore their understanding of character. Ask students working in groups or pairs to select a character from the novel. Give them five minutes to list what they feel that character would have in their handbag or in their pockets. Ask each group to read out their list without revealing the name of the character. Can the rest of the class guess the character? What clues did they use?

8. Status update

This starter combines a recap of events and exploration of character. Ask students to choose a character from the novel and imagine that they have recently updated their social network status. What would it say? What does their status show us about the character and their thoughts on the events in the novel?

9. **In their shoes**

   This is useful if a character in last lesson's reading found themselves in a difficult situation – moral, physical or emotional. Ask students to put themselves in the character's shoes: what would they do? Give students five minutes in a pair or group (the discussion element is important here) to suggest at least two pieces of advice they would give the character.

10. **Three wishes**

    This is another opportunity to recap character and events. Ask students to select a character. If that character had three wishes at this point in the novel, what would they be? Ask students to feed back one wish at a time and the rest of the class can guess whose wish it is. Follow up with a discussion of what this wish shows about the character and the situation they are in.

Reading

Comprehension

You may feel that some of this guide falls under the heading of 'The Glaringly Obvious'. You ain't seen nothing yet.

This section is about how important it is that your students understand the novel you are studying. (I told you it was obvious. But that doesn't mean it's happening in your classroom – or mine.)

Comprehension, meaning the act of understanding, is perhaps something we take for granted. The students read the text, the students had the text read to them, the students even answered a couple of questions on the text: they *must* understand the text.

Mustn't they?

No, not necessarily. Have you ever sat in a lesson, a lecture or an Inset when the teacher asks the group if they understand?

We all nod – even if we switched off ten minutes ago because we had no idea what they were talking about. Why? Because admitting you have no understanding whatsoever is embarrassing. It means one of three things:

1. You're stupid.
2. You weren't listening.
3. You're stupid and you weren't listening.

So we keep quiet and nod.

The same is happening in your classroom. No matter how much you dance and sing, blow those whistles and ring those bells, you will never have 100% of your students' concentration 100% of the time. Never.

Yet your greatest weapon when teaching the novel to reluctant readers is keeping them hooked on the plot. But it's not possible to enthuse and engage students in a story that they no longer understand or when the significance of characters is long lost. Once students lose the plot (literally), it's gone unless you pull it back within one lesson.

So without boring them rigid, you need to briefly recap the plot at the start of each lesson. Get an ever-rotating variety of students to do this for you.

It's also good to check understanding at the end of reading. A quiz on the key narrative points is not only a good way for you to assess understanding, but it can also reinforce, refresh or, in some cases, create the understanding that didn't quite happen during the reading itself.

If you don't have access to the quizzes on the ActiveTeach accompanying each *HEROES* title, get the students to write a five-question quiz for a partner. Or if students are working in two teams, get each team to write questions for the other team. The questions they set may reveal as much about their understanding as the answers do. Take note of any plot points that seem to be a source of confusion and clarify them; then reiterate this questioning and reinforcement in the next lesson before reading on.

Finally, don't shy away from activities that involve students extracting character and plot information from the narrative: summaries, fact files, maps, mind maps, family trees (all of which are covered in more detail elsewhere in this guide). These kinds of activities are central to reinforcing students' understanding of the story – and reinforcing their awareness of their understanding. In other words, you're reminding them that they are competent, successful readers.

Vocabulary

> Having a low vocabulary can trap children in a vicious circle, since children who cannot read more advanced texts miss out on opportunities to extend their vocabulary.

The act of reading is a complex synthesis of skills – but the key factor that can most powerfully help or hinder its development is, perhaps, vocabulary.

The DCSF's report, *Teaching Effective Vocabulary* (2008), compellingly summarises a range of research:

> *Vocabulary is a strong indicator of reading success (Biemiller, 2003). It was established in the 1970s that children's declining reading comprehension compared to more able peers from age 8 onwards largely resulted from a lack of vocabulary knowledge (Becker, 1977), and that this was primarily caused by a lack of learning opportunities, not a lack of natural ability. Chall et al (1990) also found that disadvantaged students showed declining reading comprehension as their narrow vocabulary limited what they could understand from texts. Having a low vocabulary can trap children in a vicious circle, since children who cannot read more advanced texts miss out on opportunities to extend their vocabulary (Fisher and Blachnowicz, 2005).*

(*Teaching Effective Vocabulary*, DCSF, 2008)

When the reluctant reader cannot decipher meaning because of a lack of vocabulary, the possibility of comprehension becomes a distant and unattainable goal and the prejudice against reading (textism?) is reinforced.

How do you know which words in your chosen novel are not being recognised?

You can try telling students that they *must* ask if there is a word on the page that they don't know, but they will almost certainly ignore you – and ignore the unknown word. Like a man with a medical problem, they'll just hope it goes away. And sure enough, when you turn the page, it will.

If it's embarrassment that's stopping their drawing attention to their ignorance, you could suggest that they surreptitiously look the word up in a dictionary in their own time. But they (almost) never will: why would someone with an entrenched dislike of books go to the largest, scariest, wordiest book they can imagine?

There is no real way to be absolutely sure that every student has understood every word you have read. Your best guide to the words that need work is your own experience and expertise: your sense that there is a word that these students might not know – a sense that your students can either confirm or prove wrong.

But if the odd word here and there is not understood by all and the narrative momentum seems to be carrying them through, does it matter?

Yes and no. Although holding students' interest in the book is paramount in developing them as readers, explicit work on vocabulary can give students a real sense of their developing reading skills and an explicit sense that you, as a teacher, are supporting them.

When you come across a word that a significant majority of students do not recognise, you can pick and choose from the following sequence of activities.

- Ask students to guess the meaning based on its context or a 'family resemblance' to another known word. (More on inference follows in the next section.)

- Give an explicit definition of the word (this in itself will be forgotten within minutes if you don't build on it).

- Develop your definition by modelling use of the word in a range of contexts.

- Ask students to suggest words with similar or related meanings, then, if applicable, rank them on the board. For example, synonyms for the word *petrified,* ranked in order, might look something like:

  1. worried
  2. scared
  3. terrified
  4. 'petrified'.

- Illustrating each word with 'emoticons' or similar doodles can help reinforce meaning. (Get a willing student involved if you don't feel ready to unleash your artwork on the world.)

- Add new vocabulary to a 'word wall' display – partly for reinforcement and partly for future reference.

When you've built up a reasonable collection on the word wall, you can open a lesson or two with a vocabulary starter:

- playing Pictionary[7] (for the visual learners) or charades (for the kinaesthetically inclined) with words from the word wall;

- asking students a question using the word – for example, *name three things that would petrify you.*

Whether you want to spend time exploring a particular word or vocabulary family depends on a number of things. Is it a significant feature of the novel you're reading – or a significant word in any context, the kind of word you feel your students should know? Will its exploration break the narrative spell that you have worked so hard to build up? Or are your students so firmly in the palm of your hand and the grip of the narrative that their interest will survive the diversion? This can only be your choice, made in the moment.

---

[7] Suggested rules of Pictionary: Divide the class into two teams. Ask a student from one team to select a word from the word wall and secretly write it on a piece of paper, which is then handed to you. He now has one minute to produce a drawing on the whiteboard from which the rest of his team must guess the word. If the word is guessed within 30 seconds, award two points; if guessed within one minute award one point. Give each team two or three goes each.

Inference

If you're reading this book, it's likely that your skills of inference are highly tuned – to the point that you don't really notice when you are using it. Yet inference is perhaps the most significant skill dividing the 'functional' reader from the 'competent' reader.

The DCSF-commissioned literature review *Effective Teaching of Inference Skills for Reading* (2008) noted:

> *A key finding of the review was that the ability to draw inferences predetermines reading skills: that is, poor inferencing causes poor comprehension and not vice versa.*

Though generally able to decode text, the reluctant reader is not always able to extract its full meaning when some of it is implied rather than explicitly stated.

You can practise this skill with your students in a starter or two. Present them with a series of short sentences in which the choice of verb suggests the subject's mood. Ask your students to 'name that mood'. For example:

- He smiled. (happy)

- He growled. (angry)

- He screamed. (frightened or in pain)

Get your students to explore their own ability to imply meaning. Ask them to choose a particular mood and write it somewhere secretly, e.g. at the back of their exercise book.

Then ask them to write a couple of sentences describing a person who is in that mood. The sentence should describe:

- how they enter the room;

- something they do on entering the room;

- something they say on entering the room;

- a word describing how they say it.

Give students model sentences for support, e.g. *He stormed into the room, picked up a chair and threw it at the window. "I'm going to kill you," he snarled.*

The underlining suggests the words and phrases that students can change to match their chosen mood. After they have written their sentences, ask students to swap and try to infer the mood their partner was suggesting.

You can use similar activities to practise a range of implications other than mood. For example:

- Information about setting, time and place: 'The sun rose...', 'The waves lapped quietly on the beach...'

- Information about the writer's attitude to a setting: 'It was dark and cold and shadows filled every corner...', 'The sky darkened and rain began to fall...'

- Information about what a character is doing: 'He slammed on the brakes...', 'He clicked the mouse and stared intently at the screen...'

- Information about one character's attitude to another: 'He rolled his eyes...', 'He tutted loudly...'

These kind of isolated, out-of-context activities are good for introducing the concept of inference, but the most valuable work is done in the context of the novel the class is reading.

For example, identify a key sentence from the chapter you are about to read – one from which significant plot or character information may be inferred. Present it to the class with a significant word removed and ask students to guess the missing word based on context.

As students' confidence in their inference skills grows, increase your demands. After reading a chapter, take as many opportunities as you can bear to return to examples requiring use of inference from the reader. Highlight all the language choices that carry inferential meaning and ask students to identify what is being implied.

For example: *Ben wandered through the school gates, whistling quietly to himself. The playground was empty. He was late again.*

Question students on the use of:

- *wandered* (he doesn't seem to care that he's late)

- *whistling* (he is happy and carefree)

- *empty* (is he late? or early? or perhaps it's Sunday?)

- *again* (he's often late).

Two key things to remember:

- Don't interrupt your reading (and the accumulation of narrative meaning) to work on inference. Do it before or after reading.

- Before asking students to do it, model the process of inference by thinking aloud: show students how you infer meaning from the clues that the writer has left.

And when you feel you have 'done' inference to death (and beyond), remember: you are not just developing an essential reading skill, you're also confirming meaning. It isn't an analysis of the writer's linguistic technique; it's an assurance of your students' understanding. And as noted previously (and repeatedly), your students' understanding is paramount in their growing confidence as competent readers.

Mains

Fun

Reading a novel in class should be fun – fun for your students and fun for you. In fact, like so much of school life, it should be more fun for them than for you.

The real fun should be in the story – and it's up to you to revel in the pleasure of a good story well told and hope your feverish excitement becomes contagious.

Forget the finer points of language and structure: short sentences to build tension, active verbs to create pace and excitement. The first job is to get your students to remember that there *can* be some tension, pace and excitement in a story. The technicalities can come later.

Two considerations should guide your planning for reluctant readers:

1. Will students find the activity fun (hopefully beginning to make some association between the words 'fiction' and 'fun')?

2. Will it help students engage in, understand and enjoy the novel?

If your planned activity achieves one of these, then do it. If it achieves both, then congratulate yourself and tell everyone you know.

Getting it straight

In the early stages of reading a novel, it's essential that your students are really clear about the names, relationships, situations and backgrounds of the key characters.

If students have a solid foundation of understanding, they will engage with the story and build on their understanding much more quickly and easily as the narrative develops. Here are some suggestions to get that essential information cemented in your students' heads:

1. **Making it tangible**

   This is a valuable activity to clarify students' thinking and to reassure you of their understanding. It is also a useful reference for students as you progress through the story.

   If the novel on which you are working focuses on a family, ask students to draw a family tree, no matter how simplistic this might seem.

   If your novel is about a specific location, ask students to use the knowledge they have gained from the early chapters and/or their imagination to draw a map.

   If both character and location are relevant, ask students to combine the two. Students can then start to add to their understanding of characters with images and symbols as well as language.

For example, a visual representation of the characters and setting established in the first couple of chapters of *Ghost Game* might look something like Figure 2.

As characters' likes, dislikes and relationships emerge during the course of the novel, ask students to add notes and images to the 'picture'.

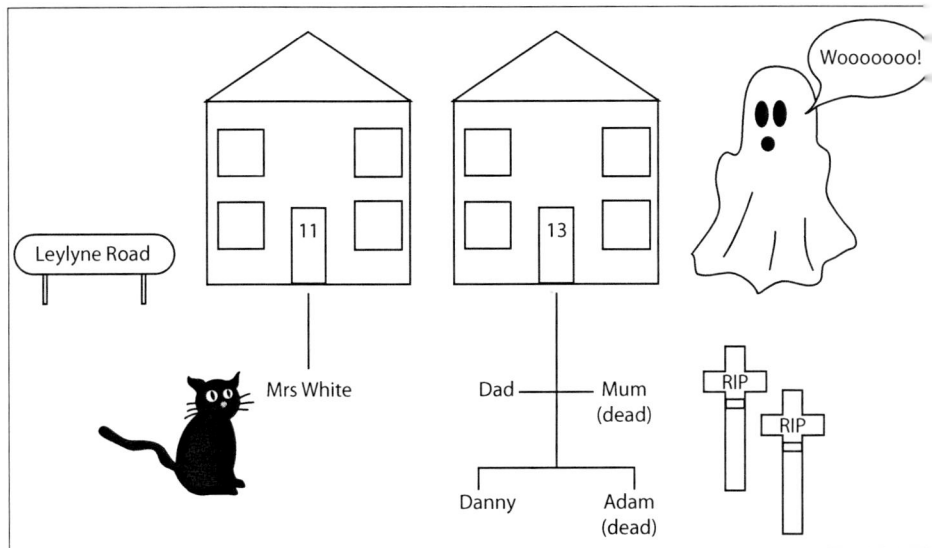

Figure 2: A visual representation of the characters and setting in the opening chapters of *Ghost Game*.

2. Fact files

Fact files on specific characters, or even social network profiles, can help students compile their knowledge of a particular character – and help you assess their reading and comprehension.

Ask students to re-read the initial chapter(s) of the novel and gather as much information as they can about their (or your) chosen character. Providing a template fact file for students to complete gives them a guide to the information to look out for. See Figure 3 below for an example of a fact file for the character of Luke Kitson in *i-SSASSINS*.

Worksheet: Fact file on Luke Kitson	
Real name:	
Age:	
Family background:	
Education:	
Skills:	
Now known as:	
Age:	
Address:	
Financial status:	
Known crimes:	

Figure 3: A sample fact file worksheet

Drama

What better way to get some kinaesthetic learning into your lesson than through drama? But there are some ground rules that need to be established at your very first mention of the word 'drama':

- **The call to silence.** This could be you clapping, raising a hand high above your head or thumping your desk with a stapler – but your students need to know what it means and act quickly on it. In most cases the threat to end the activity immediately is enough to make only the first attempt a near failure.

- **No physical contact.** Even if students insist on placing the noble arts of fist fighting or jujitsu at the heart of their drama work (and they almost certainly will), they need to be clear that this must not involve actual fighting.

- **Be an audience.** Your students already know how a good audience should behave. The preparation time you allocated was for preparing their performance – not when they are supposed to be watching someone else's. Insist on silence and respectful enthusiasm.

- **No ties round the head.** If your school uniform features a tie, insist that your students do not remove it from their neck and tie it round their heads. Why? The same reason that the letter 'i' should not have a heart for a dot. It's visually repulsive and unacceptable on almost every level. The same goes for stuffing other kids' jumpers up their own to make them look like a fat person.

Some classic drama activities

There are many drama activities which you can adapt to your chosen text in numerous ways. Here are just some that are easily managed and productive:

1. Charades

- The mime-based guessing game can be adapted to explore character or to visualise key episodes from the novel.

- Divide students into two or more teams. Write the names of either key characters or key episodes from the novel on pieces of paper. Give them to random members of each team. Their task is to use only mime to communicate the words on the piece of paper to their team within a specific time limit – say, 30 seconds for two points, or one minute for one point. Emphasise that there should be no speaking during the actual mime, either from the guessers or the mimer. You will 'stop the clock' after 30 seconds and ask the team for their guess – and again at the end of one minute. Be clear that you will deduct points for *any* noise during the mime.

- This is useful for discussing character or plot in the post-charade analysis of the clues that helped the guessers.

2. Freeze frames/Sculpture

- Divide students into groups of three or four. Ask them to spend five to ten minutes choosing an incident from the novel that they feel is the tensest, the funniest or simply the best in the novel – and ask them to recreate it as a frozen image, a living illustration.

- Can the rest of the class guess which part of the novel is being illustrated? Who represents which character? What visual clues were used? The real value here is in the preliminary preparation, engaging students in discussion and in the novel.

- Add an additional element of collaboration by pairing groups: Group A have to 'sculpt' Group B into their chosen image using only verbal instructions – and without naming any of the characters or actions that will give the game away. Group B then 'sculpt' Group A.

3. Hot-seating

- Hot-seating involves one person taking on the role of a character from the novel and responding to questions from the class.

- You need at least one confident student – and preferably three or four – to take on the daunting hot seat. And you may feel that you don't have one. If so, I'm afraid the only recourse is for you to take on the job – which is the most enormous incentive for students to engage with the task. Sir/Miss is going to play 'Let's Pretend'!

- Give students ten minutes to prepare three to five questions to ask your chosen character – and to note down the answers they would give if they were in the hot seat. Emphasise that you may ask students to read out their answers and they should be prepared to justify them.

4. **Conscience alley**

- One student (or teacher) takes on a nominal role as a character from the novel at a point of emotional or moral difficulty.

- Ask students to write down just one thought that would be in this character's head as they face this dilemma.

- Students form two rows about a metre apart: an alley down which the 'character' will walk. As the student representing the character walks past them, students speak aloud the 'thought' they have prepared.

- Point out to students that it doesn't matter if their 'thought' is similar to another's – it just emphasises how important their idea is at this point in the novel. (Point this out just before beginning the walk – not before the preparation, or they'll all say the same thing.)

- You can reduce students' self-consciousness by getting them to write their thought down. You can then take them in and randomly redistribute them so each student is given someone else's 'thought' to read aloud. It might be a good idea to get students to put their name on the piece of paper too, just in case somebody thinks it's hilarious to write something obscene.

- Optionally, the student in the character role then takes the hot seat and voices an action they will take in the face of this dilemma.

5. TV news

- As a more active version of writing a newspaper article, ask students to prepare the television news bulletin reporting an incident from the novel. Groups of four or five can take on the roles of the newsreader, the reporter and two or three characters to interview.

- Make it clear that students should present a polished improvisation and not write a script in an exercise book that they then pass labouredly around during a painfully halting performance.

6. Chat show

- Students take on the roles of interviewer and characters from the novel, discussing the events and their actions in the novel. Whether it's *Newsnight* or Jeremy Kyle style may be dictated by your choice of text. Again, a polished improvisation is what you're after.

Putting it in a context

For the majority of their school day, students know exactly what is expected of them. They are children; they should behave; they should work hard; they should succeed. As students get older, the opportunities for play – for forgetting who you are and what you should be – get more and more rare.

Drama is one opportunity students have for stretching their imagination. But you can apply the same level of 'play' to their reading and writing: by placing it in an imaginative context, a scenario in which they become someone else entirely, taking on the life, thoughts, actions or purposes of someone who isn't a student in a school, expected to do their work because the teacher has asked them to.

Once you have established the learning objective in your mind, it's simply a question of deciding how you will present the activity.

If you want students to write a script based on an event from the novel, send them a letter from a major film studio explaining that the film version of the novel is about to be made and inviting them to submit a script for consideration. The same goes for storyboarding the film trailer or designing the film poster or merchandise.

If you want them to produce a piece of drama inspired by the novel, send them another letter from the same major film studio inviting them to audition.

If you want them to produce a piece of extended writing – an extra chapter or an idea for the sequel – send them a letter from the publishers explaining that the original author is too busy and inviting them to submit their ideas.

If you want students to extract key facts about a character, give them a reason to do so. Place them in the employment of the novel's villain who demands that they produce a dossier on this character in the next hour – or face the consequences.

If you want them to use clues from the text to predict how the mystery will pan out, cast them as detectives. Send them a memo from their Chief of Police asking them to study the clues and report their theories in the next 30 minutes.

If you want them to write a character profile of the novel's villain, cast them as forensic psychologists specialising in criminal profiling (which might take a little explaining, but mention serial killers once or twice and you'll have their undivided attention).

Maintain the scenario in every element of the task, whether it's in supporting sentence starters...

I was proceeding in a westerly direction in the course of my police duties when it came to my attention that...

I noticed the suspect was...

...or in your presentation:

TOP SECRET

S.M.A.S.H.

To all agents

Your leader needs to know all the facts about _____. Compile a dossier on his past, his activities, and his known associates and have it on my desk in the next 30 minutes – or face the consequences.

Agent X

It may seem like you are simply dressing up a straightforward activity in a deceptively fancy costume. That's because you are. Students may even rumble this and accuse you of child-like pretence. But they'll still tackle the activity with the enthusiasm of a child at play.

Empathy

Encouraging students to work from a point of empathy with a character is similar to framing a task within an imaginative context, yet more immersive.

You are not simply asking students to write about a character; you are asking them to *become* that character.

The starting point for this should be discussion, linking the character's experience to that of your students. At a significant point in the character's experience, ask your students to put themselves in this character's shoes. Begin by identifying what kind of shoes he or she would choose to wear. Trainers? Wellies? Stilettos?

How would your students feel if this (whatever it might be) had happened to them? How do your students think the character feels about the situation? Have any of your students ever felt like that? When?

We frequently ask students to write empathetically, writing in the first person and taking on the voice of a character. The diary entry is the standard. But why is this character writing a diary? Is their diary habit mentioned in the novel? Do students have any experience of writing a diary – or a burning desire to acquire any?

If this seems unlikely to you, then rethink the context: what (and why) would this character write expressing their innermost thoughts – and to whom? A social network comment to one of the other characters? An email? A text message? A confession to the police?

If none of these suits the situation, then reposition the character in the film adaptation: give students the scenario of the character sitting on a park bench or lying in bed, contemplating their life. Ask students to write a monologue, the voiceover of the character's thoughts as they ponder their difficulties. The echoing voiceover while the camera focuses on a furrowed brow is not, perhaps, as common a cinematic trope as it once was, but students are considerably more familiar with it than the diary form.

And you'll never have to correct the words 'Dear Dairy' again.

Speaking and listening

For any reader, independent reading is a solitary activity. For the reluctant reader struggling to make sense of a text, this independence can become isolation. If the text cannot be made to make sense, the reader will soon walk away from it. This is just one reason why discussion of the text is so vital for the reluctant reader (as previously discussed: see *The value of talk*, page 11).

Whole class discussion

Opportunities for whole class discussion should be actively sought: anything that encourages students to reflect on the story and its characters, anything that engages them in the text and its relevance to their own experience.

Some students have been known to consider getting the teacher into extended discussion to be a kind of diversionary game: if we can get him/her talking, we might not have to do the writing s/he mentioned at the start of the lesson. Welcome the distraction.

Unsurprisingly, 'why' and 'how' questions are the best prompts to discussion:

- Why did he do that? What do you think?

- How do you think she feels?

- How did it make you feel?

- Why do you think the writer decided to...?

Beware, though, of your four or five most vociferous students dominating the discussion. There will always be those who can't stop talking – and those who can't start. Make it clear to your students that you want and expect to hear from them: in the same way that you would not tolerate students abstaining from a writing task, you expect them to take part in discussion; you expect to hear from every student at least once every two or three lessons; and you will do everything you can to support them in this.

For example:

- Give students two or three minutes to consider the point of discussion – time to gather and note down their thoughts before you ask for contributions.

- Don't wait for quieter students to put their hand up; invite specific students to contribute their thoughts.

- Draw the quietest students into participating with a hands-up vote: who thinks this character should react in this way? And who thinks in that way? Ask quieter students to expand on the reasons for their voting decision.

Group discussion

Group discussion is one of the most valuable reading activities and one of the most difficult to manage.

The moment you announce group work, the silent(ish) diplomacy of group formation begins. Students start gesturing and looking imploringly at each other. When this begins, you're in danger of losing them. Make it clear that you will be telling them in a moment what groups they will be in – but that they must first listen to the task you want them to complete.

It's important that students feel comfortable with their fellow group members. While friendship groups are the quickest way to get students drifting off-task, non-friendship groups can be the quickest way to an awkward and unproductive silence. The decision to group by gender, ability, friendship or otherwise has to be a decision driven by the promotion of discussion, some of which will, you must accept, be unproductive.

There are a number of ways to keep talk as productive as possible:

- Set a strict time limit on the discussion and clearly count down the time remaining.

- Give a specific outcome that you expect from the discussion at the end of the time available – preferably a short written outcome to focus students on completing the task and reaching a conclusion. This should probably be no more than two or three sentences. Give students sentence starters to support and direct the outcome, e.g.

We think that *this character* should:

1. _____

2. _____

3. _____

- Provide students with a series of prompts to structure their discussion. So if you're asking students to discuss how a character can resolve a difficult situation, avoid simply asking, 'What do you think this character should do next?'. Instead, provide a prompt sheet outlining all the different elements of the situation that need to be considered. For example:
  - the causes of the situation;
  - characters whose feelings need to be taken into account;
  - characters who can help the situation;
  - the possible options among which the character must choose.

Be clear on the rules of group work before you begin: better still, ask them to tell you the rules so you can note them on the board for reference during the activity. This is your best chance to pre-empt disputes and create productive harmony. You should end up with a list that looks something like:

- Everyone should contribute.

- It's the whole group's responsibility to ensure that the whole group contributes.

- Listen to each other.

- Respect everyone's ideas.

- If you disagree, explain why – and explain why you feel your idea is better – but if no one agrees, put up with the majority verdict cheerfully.

- Try to resolve disputes within the group; only when this is not possible, call the teacher.

When the time is up, ask each group to feed back their conclusions, emphasising that you expect everyone's full attention during feedback. As part of their feedback, ask each group to comment on the quality of their group work: did they all abide by the rules that you (or they) outlined at the start of the activity? Praise students for the quality of their outcome *and* the quality of the process.

Reluctant readers are frequently reluctant writers. For these students, talk is the most accessible way they have of reflecting on your chosen text, the million-word-mountain you have put in front of them. It helps them assimilate, consider, explore and empathise. As such, you may find speaking and listening should become your first choice of activity, not a statutory obligation to be squeezed in (or out) at some point.

Writing

Reluctant readers are often reluctant writers. But luckily you're concentrating on improving reading skills, so the only writing tasks you really need to worry about are those that support your students' reading.

These should follow some simple guidelines:

- Keep it short.

- Keep it focused.

- Keep the task embedded in, or inspired by, students' reading of the novel.

- Provide plenty of support.

- Make it readily and easily assessable.

1. Keep it short

Extended writing amid your reading of the novel should be considered by your students as an interruption. If you have succeeded in getting them into the book, they should resent you taking them away from it. So aim for writing tasks that can be completed in 20 minutes or less.

You don't need your students to write a three-page letter in role as the novel's protagonist in order to assess whether students have empathised with his thoughts and feelings. Get your students to write a social network status update or a text message to a friend (perhaps another character from the novel or an imagined friend). Take feedback verbally and you will know instantly whether they have engaged with the character and the novel.

Make brevity a virtue: set writing tasks that must be completed in 15 words or fewer. For example:

- a summary of the chapter you have just read

- the one piece of advice you would give the character in a tricky situation

- predicting what happens next

- summing up a character from the novel.

2. Keep it focused

Be clear on the purpose, the objective of the task, and strip away all that is unnecessary.

If you want students to respond imaginatively to the novel, don't ask them to write the novel's sequel – just a summary plan of the plot.

If you want students to use descriptive language, don't ask them to write a lengthy description – just a mind map of the descriptive language they might use.

A review? Two things I liked, two things I didn't like.

3. Keep the task embedded

Bearing in mind that a writing task can become a distraction from reading, aim to keep any writing tied as closely to the novel as possible. Avoid thematically linked tasks (*Stone Cold*/homelessness, *Holes*/crime-and-punishment spring to mind). Keep your students' minds firmly in the world of the novel. See *Empathy*, page 70.

The best writing tasks are those that ask students to express a personal response to the novel and allow them the space to express it. This is a list of questions (from Richard Peck's 'Ten Questions to Ask About a Novel') which can be very effective as whole class discussion starters or as a stimulus for short-burst writing:

1. What would this story be like if the main character were of the opposite sex?

2. Why is the story set where it is?

3. If you were to make a film of this story, which characters would you eliminate if you couldn't use them all?

4. Would you film this story in black and white or colour?

5. How is the main character different from you?

6. Why or why not would this story make a good TV series?

7. What's one thing in the story that's happened to you?

8. Reread the first paragraph of Chapter 1. What's in it to make you read on?

81

9. If you had to design a new cover for the book, what would it look like?

10. What does the title tell you about the book? Does it tell the truth?

4. Provide plenty of support

Whole class planning on the board, planning charts, modelling, paragraph subheadings, whole class vocabulary gathering sessions, sentence starters... the possible means of support are virtually endless. Collapse will occur long before you have exhausted them. For most shorter writing tasks, some scaffolding, some modelling and some sentence starters should just about do it.

5. Make it readily and easily assessable

Bearing in mind that you're assessing your students' reading, not their writing, most of these short tasks can be broadly assessed verbally. And when you do come to assess individual students' work more closely, asking yourself one question should be enough to assess whether the task has been successfully completed: is this student demonstrating his engagement with the novel? This is, of course, something of a gross simplification – but it should be the key aim of every writing task you set.

IT and multimedia resources

The English classroom is not always the most technologically advanced arena in which to create a multisensory, multimedia experience. Getting the video to work can be enough of a challenge. But there are some relatively easy ways to add some visual sparkle to your chosen novel.

Images

(See also *Starters* on page 37.)

A lack of prior knowledge can be a severe hindrance in reading. If your students cannot visualise a setting (or an object or event) because it is entirely alien to them, it can severely impede a novel's relevance to them and their engagement with it. Do your students know what central London looks like? Or a walled Roman fort in Ancient Britain? If not, show them an image from the internet – or get your students to find you one.

Ask your students to respond to the novel through images. A mood board or collage of images and words that the novel suggests to them can be a highly effective way for students to respond to the narrative and its characters and themes.

Prompt a visual response to the novel with some initial questioning:

- What colours do you think should be used on the cover of this novel? An adventure novel might be black and red, for example. A mystery story perhaps grey and purple.

- How would you sum up the novel in a single object? It could be the smallest household item or an entire building.

- If you were making the film of the novel, in which season or type of weather would you set it? Is it a miserably rainy novel, a happy, sunny novel or a dramatically stormy novel?

Go on to explain that students' collages should not be just a picture of an object and a cumulus nimbus on a coloured background. It could also include:

- images of people who you think look like the characters in the novel

- images of places, events, things that are relevant to the novel

- words that are important in the mood or action of the novel

- anything that reflects your feelings about the story.

Music

Music is often the least relevant medium to the reading of a novel – but it is probably a central part of your students' lives. Remind students of recent films that have featured songs as their theme tune – or ask them to remind you. What song would they choose for the theme tune of the film based on this novel?

You can extend this to developing the original soundtrack album: what five pieces of music would students choose for five key moments in the film?

Film

Students are always delighted when you promise that you'll be watching the feature film adaptation when you've finished reading the novel (but only if one has actually been made, otherwise it can backfire on you).

Some might argue that 'watching the video' is nothing more than an empty treat, something to keep the class quiet at the end of a long term. And they'd have a point. But it can be a perfect way to wrap up the whole reading experience: an audio-visual reinforcement that they enjoyed the book, they enjoyed the film, they enjoyed the story.

But why wait until you've finished the novel? Whet students' appetites with the first ten minutes or so of the film once you're more than a little way into the novel. It can be an excellent prompt to discussion of character (did you think he looked/acted/spoke like that?). Do repeatedly remind students that the image of this character that *they* have in *their* minds is the real one – because that's the one that was created by the author. And the film is just a pale imitation.

If a film hasn't been made of the novel, look for a film connected by genre or subject matter. How do the two stories being told – one on paper, one on film – compare? Are they similar or different? Is the reader's/viewer's reaction likely to be the same?

Some film-related activities benefit from there being no film version available: students cannot have seen it already and so have to produce their own response rather than one strongly reminiscent of Hollywood's. For example:

- Storyboard the trailer for the film of the novel, selecting key moments to get the audience desperate to book their seats. Include details of music, dialogue, voiceover and captions. Watch the trailer from a recent or forthcoming blockbuster for inspiration – available from the Internet Movie Database *(www.imdb.com)*.

- Cast the film, choosing actors from film or television for the main roles.

- Write the tagline or slogan for the advertising campaign. Again, find some recent examples for inspiration from *www.imdb.com*.

IT

The internet is an astonishing resource for students to gather information and images in response to a novel (if you can keep them off the mini games sites). Word processing and desktop publishing programs can transform the appearance of students' work – and their pride in that work.

But consider the internet not just as a resource but as a medium. Get students exploring websites created to promote recent novels then ask them to design and write the website for your novel. It can feature a blurb (without giving too much away), character profiles, games, competitions – in fact anything your students think would keep visitors clicking. Or you could ask students to design and write a website for one of the characters or an organisation featured in the novel.

––––––––––––

I must confess that I sometimes find myself shuffling uncomfortably when using these kinds of activity in the classroom. I tell myself that they lack rigour and gravitas. It's just colouring in, I mumble awkwardly to myself. It's just keeping them busy, I mutter.

But then I look again: at students actively engaged in exploring their response to a piece of fiction.

Displays

Picture a primary school classroom – bright and bustling with wall displays, things dangling from the ceiling, a technicolour assault.

Now picture your classroom – and compare.

Two things may spring to mind:

1. Oh dear.[8]

2. No time.

A beautiful display in the primary classroom is, dare I say it, easier to achieve. The same students are in the same room every day, churning out art and DT on a weekly basis, producing lovely things to make lovely displays. They don't have to share the room with three different maths classes and a science lesson that had to go in there because all the labs were full – none of whom see it as their classroom and so have little respect for it.

But the value of classroom display is vast and a chore well worth its weight. Students love to see their work on display. Even those who sneer with disinterest are secretly looking out of the corner of one eye (even as they're rolling it skywards) and feeling a little pinch of pride somewhere deep down.

---

[8] Apologies if your classroom is a thing of beauty. Mine frequently isn't.

Displaying a student's work tells them you value the piece of work, you value the work they put into it and you value them. It creates a learning environment that proudly announces to whom this workspace belongs and their values. And if you can get students to do the bulk of the putting up, then so much the better.

Before you start your novel, clear as much display space as you can. Put a notice above it, announcing whose work this is (or will be) and on which novel. Tell your students that they will be filling this space.

Start filling it as soon as possible. Don't worry that there are yawning gaps to begin with. Pin up an 'under construction' or 'coming soon' sign.

Ideally, every student should be fairly equally represented on the display. But don't just pin up everything and anything: students need to know that you're not just putting up any old thing; they need to see that their work has been judged by a discriminating eye and been passed beautiful enough for the viewing public.

Work from left to right, dividing displays of different tasks with a thin paper border – and label each section as a record of the work you have been doing.

Don't wait for storyboards and illustrations to pin up. Get students to type up and print out those short-burst writing activities in big bold font: the text message, the status updates, or a prediction of what happens next.[9] Cover the walls in them. And don't forget to save a space for your vocabulary 'word wall'.

If it all sounds rather tiring, that's because it is – or rather it can be. So get the students to do it. If you've got a student who can be trusted with a staple gun under careful supervision, use them. Don't type and print your own notices and labels. The only bit that you should be doing is selecting the work to go up. Hand it over to a small team of trustees (hopefully a rotating team of willing volunteers) and give them the last 10–15 minutes of a lesson (or even a lunchtime if they're really enthused) and tell them to get busy.

As the display fills up, students will come to regard filling every last inch as a challenge to be met. And this patchwork of your students' hard graft will stand both as a record of achievement and as something to reflect on and refer to: a reminder of the last time you did something similar and a model for students to aspire to – or even exceed.

---

[9] Make sure your students save any work they do on a computer – and print two copies: one for display and one for a possible portfolio of work – see *Assessment* on page 95.

Homework

The reluctant reader and – as already presupposed – reluctant writer may well be a reluctant homeworker to boot.

One incentive that you can draw on is the team competition. Not only will you be awarding points for the best homework (and that could be all of them), but you will be adding bonus points if the whole team does their homework on time. Or, if you're feeling particularly ruthless, you could threaten to withhold all points for homework unless the whole team has completed it on time.

Assuming that your reluctant readers' homework record has been patchy at its peak, you need to tailor your demands accordingly. Nothing too big, nothing too daunting, and preferably something appealing: in fact something very much like the work you have been doing in lessons. Short-burst writing activities, visual responses and so on.

One option is to set a long-term project for homework: design the website promoting the novel, for example. If you do this, break it down into manageable, bitesize chunks: the Games page this week, the Author FAQs page next week and so on – and monitor students' progression, taking the work in on a weekly basis (and getting it up on that display board). Otherwise you'll get to the end of the novel and find that some of them decided to save up the homework for the night before the deadline only to find there was something unmissable on the telly, or it was their mum's birthday, or the dog had to be rushed to the vet, or all three.

Assessment

The mantra of this guide (and the entire *HEROES* project) is to engage readers in fiction, build their confidence and so bring improvement.

The traditional model of assessment is, of course, intended to measure improvement. You may well be obliged by school policy to assess your students' progress – probably with a National Curriculum (NC) level. So the first task is to identify some kind of reading assessment that will allow your students to show what they have learned.

You could give them a formal essay: a character study of the main character or a particularly interesting supporting character (the villain of the piece, for example). See the exemplar planning worksheet on page 97. Emphasise the importance of students demonstrating their inference skills – a significant feature of higher NC levels.

If you don't want to drag your students through this kind of final assessment – and, as their last piece of work on this novel, it could quite easily sour any taste for fiction they might have acquired – get your students to put together a portfolio of work that they have completed during the course of the novel. You will need to direct them on the best pieces to include: pieces which, all together, show their awareness of character and of plot, the writer's language choices, viewpoint and intention, their skills of inference, and so on across as broad a range of assessment focuses as possible.

When you return their work, lavish praise upon them. Don't reveal their National Curriculum level. While you may be proud of the progress in reading and in attitude that they have made – and they may feel they have climbed a mountain. They may not see their progression from a Level 4b to a Level 4a as fair recompense. And all your good work is undone.

But there are two ways of looking at the work you have been doing and the difference you have been making. One way is through the measuring glass of formal assessment. The other – and the real measure of the objectives I am suggesting – is in examining any progress in the students' attitudes to reading.

You may feel you can identify at a glance which of your students have been engaged in the novel, grown in confidence and are in danger of reading another book. You can ask them: did you enjoy the book? A significant number of 'yes' votes is a victory.

Then you can dig deeper. Just as you surveyed students' attitudes to reading before you started the novel, you can do something similar at the end of it. This is an opportunity not only to evaluate your students' reading but the choice of novel and the ways in which you have taught it – and may help the planning of a similar mission in future years. See the suggested survey template on page 98.

Planning worksheet: Character profile			
Introduction: Who is [this character]? What does he do in the novel?			
	Point	**Evidence**	**Explanation**
PEE 1 Write about when we are first introduced to this character.			
PEE 2 Write about [a significant appearance of this character].			
PEE 3 Write about [another significant appearance of this character].			
PEE 4 Write about [a third significant appearance of this character].			
Conclusion: Sum up how you think [this character] is presented in the novel.			

Figure 4: Example planning worksheet

Teaching survey template

Your name _____

How many stars (out of five) would you give this novel? _____

Write three things you liked or didn't like about [the novel]:

1. _____

2. _____

3. _____

Write three things you liked or didn't like about the lessons:

1. _____

2. _____

3. _____

Do you think your reading has improved? Yes / Maybe / No

Why? _____

_____

_____

_____

Would you read another book by the same author or in the same genre? Explain the reasons for your answer.

_____

_____

_____

Figure 5: Teaching survey template

Beyond the classroom

Hopefully you have created some momentum in encouraging and improving your students' reading. You have guided them to the border of becoming readers. The real challenge now lies in maintaining that momentum, in taking them over the border. Tell them so. Tell them you want them to become readers – and why.

And how. Explain that the class will be spending a lesson in the library every two or three weeks, that this will be a challenge for you because you've got a vast curriculum to cover in a relatively short time – but you think it's worth it.

Explain the purpose of these library visits: to look at books and read some of them. Sweeten the pill by dividing the lesson into two sections: say, 20 minutes of free choice with quiet talk where students can read fiction, non-fiction, newspapers, magazines, whatever they like, and the boys can gather round the *Guinness Book of Records*; and the rest of the lesson either choosing or reading fiction with nothing louder than the occasional whisper.

Encourage students to begin their search with the recommendation of a friend or the advice of a helpful school librarian – suggesting they think about the kind of book they want to read *before* they ask.

To avoid students aimlessly ambling while holding a book or two, give some structure and purpose to the choosing process. Give students three things they should look at and/or read to guide their choice:

- the book cover
- the blurb on the back of the book
- the first page of Chapter 1.

For each book they pick up and vaguely like the look of, ask them to complete sentences something like this:

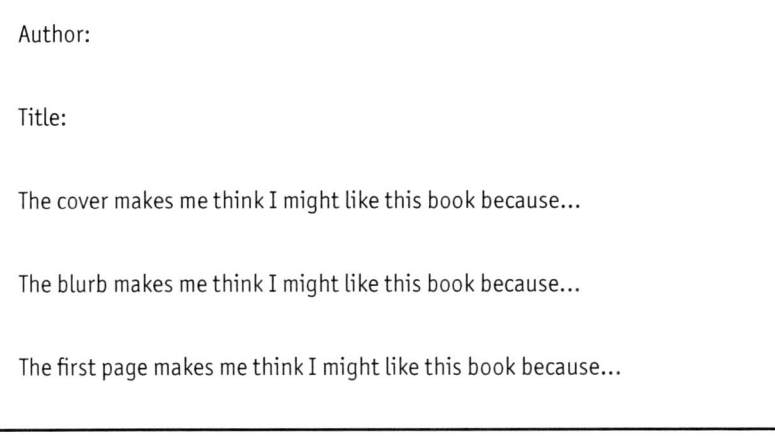

Author:

Title:

The cover makes me think I might like this book because...

The blurb makes me think I might like this book because...

The first page makes me think I might like this book because...

Figure 6: Sample student survey

At some point in the process they may decide they want to abandon the book. Be clear: there is no point in persevering with a book that you don't want to read; move on and find one you do want to read. This gives you a record of how many books they have tried and the kinds of book they are exploring.

Finally, students should also consider readability. Explain the five-finger method to students. When you start off on a new book, you hold up five fingers (either actually or metaphorically – the latter more likely) and every time you find a word you don't know you put a finger down. If by the end of the first page, all five fingers are down then that book is not the one for you.

Once they have selected a book, students need time to read. The library lesson once every two or three weeks just isn't enough. And as these are students with little or no recent history of self-initiated reading, they need you to make the time for them.

Give them ten minutes' silent reading at the start of every English lesson. If you have the luxury of a teaching assistant, ask them to listen to a student read outside the classroom, one each lesson, on strict rotation.

At the end of each silent reading session, get a student to collect the reading books in so they can stay with you in the classroom, not disappear under their bed never to be seen or read again – unless, of course, they are desperate to take their book home.

Yes, this will cut into your teaching time still further. But what better way to spend ten minutes?

Use the time to talk (quietly) to some students about their reading. Nothing too demanding, but everything entirely positive and encouraging: 'Is it any good?' or 'You're halfway through it already!' or 'You've nearly finished it, what are you going to read next?' will do nicely.

Personally, I avoid the 'book talk' where a student tells the class about the book they have been reading. If you're a reluctant speaker (and reluctant readers frequently are), then there is no greater disincentive to finishing a book than knowing you're going to have get up and speak in front of 30 people at the end of it. The fact that you, the teacher, know the student has completed the book, and has something to say about it, is enough.

Finally, see if you can get the pastoral team on your side. Some schools run a 'buddy' scheme – where older students act as role models mentoring younger students in a registration or two each week. See if you can add reading into the relationship: one in every two sessions, or half of each session, is given over to the older student listening to the younger one read. It gives focus and purpose to their interaction and provides yet another opportunity for reading improvement. No Head of Year or Deputy Head (Pastoral) could argue with that, surely?

The last word

There are a lot of words in this book. These, I think, are the most important:

- Choose your novel carefully. Choose pace, plot and character – not moral dilemmas or richness of language.

- Your real focus in this mission is reading. Forget improving their writing for now – first get them reading and talking about reading.

- Your only real teaching objective is enjoyment – theirs definitely, yours hopefully – enjoyment in the story itself and enjoyment in exploring it.

- Reading one novel is not going to improve your students' reading. It may, however, improve their attitude to reading and get them doing it more often. And that will improve their reading.

- Enjoy it.